MOVIE
MAGIC

ROBIN CROSS

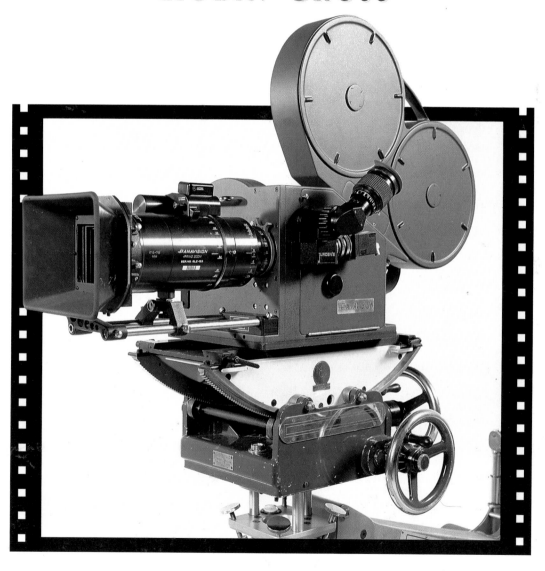

Sterling Publishing Co., Inc. New York

Designed and conceived by
S•W Books

Illustrated by
Mike Lacy, Ian Thompson,
Rob Sloane and David West

Picture research by
Brooks Krissler Research

Edited by
Diana Craig

Library of Congress Cataloging-
in-Publication Data available
10 9 8 7 6 5 4 3 2 1

Published 1995 by
Sterling Publishing Company, Inc.
387 Park Avenue South
New York
N.Y. 10016
Originally published in
Great Britain by
Simon & Schuster Young Books
Text and illustrations
© 1994 by S•W Books
Distributed in Canada by
Sterling Publishing
c/o Canadian Manda Group
One Atlantic Avenue, Suite 105
Toronto, Ontario
Canada M6K 3E7

Every effort has been made to
contact all the relevant copyright
holders and apologies are offered
for any omissions that may have
inadvertently been made.

Printed and bound
in Portugal by
Edições ASA

Sterling ISBN: 0 8069 1364 9

CONTENTS

INTRODUCTION

On February 1, 1893, the American inventor Thomas Alva Edison completed the first motion picture studio. It was a big, black hut made of wood, paper and tar, mounted on a pivot so that it could catch the sun. Later that year, Edison's film camera caught one of his assistants in the act of sneezing. *Fred Ott's Sneeze*, copyrighted in January 1894, was the very first film.

From those humble beginnings, 100 years ago, a huge worldwide industry has grown. It has enormous power to reflect what is going on in the world, to make us laugh or cry, and to shape how we think. Since the first camera rolled in Edison's studio, cinema seems to have changed beyond recognition. Yet in one important way it has not changed at all. Today's audiences experience the same kind of wonder while watching Disney's *Aladdin* or Steven Spielberg's *Jurassic Park* as they did when they saw the first crude products of the infant film business. The effects that amaze us today are created by computers rather than clumsy wooden cameras, but both bring us the magic of movies.

Meet the stars
Dotted throughout the book are small portraits of some of the more famous actors, directors and movie moguls. See if you can recognize the famous faces in the star-studded gallery.

Meet the crew
Find out who does what in the movie business. Wardrobe, focus puller, grip, director, editor and many more are all here.

How's it done?
Find out the facts behind the magic of the movies! How does Superman fly? How do they create such huge scenes? What is sensorama? Look out for the special panels that give away the secrets.

THE EARLY YEARS

Hundreds of years separate the shadow play of medieval Asian puppets (left) from the big-screen spectaculars of modern cinema. Behind them both is our fascination with pictures that move. Over 100 years ago clever little toys like the Fantascope (below) created the illusion of a moving picture by bombarding the eye with a fast succession of images. Because our eyes need time to take in what they see, the pictures merged together and moved. At the same time, the pioneers of photography were making another vital link between the world of flickering shadows on the wall and and the billion-dollar movies that are produced today.

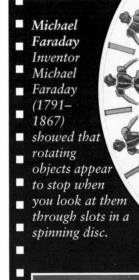

The Magic Lantern

Using a lens and a candle as a light source, the Magic Lantern projected the images from painted slides onto the wall. It is the ancestor of the movie projector.

The Thaumatrope

One of the earliest optical toys, the thaumatrope is a spinning disc with a picture on either side. When the disc spins, the bird appears in the cage.

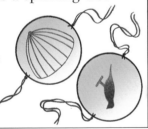

Michael Faraday Inventor Michael Faraday (1791–1867) showed that rotating objects appear to stop when you look at them through slots in a spinning disc.

Trick of the Eye

The Fantascope is a slotted disc with a series of pictures in the center. To make the pictures move, you hold the Fantascope up in front of the mirror, spin it and look through the slots.

Poetry in Motion

Eadweard Muybridge (1830–1904) was a pioneer of photography. His photographic experiments with animals and humans in motion were the link between still photography and films.

What the Butler Saw

The Mutoscope was popular in America in the 1890s. You put a coin in the slot and turned a handle. The Mutascope then quickly leafed through a set of photographs on cards, making the images on them move. Some of the sequences were very saucy for the time, even showing women undressing— hence their nickname "What the Butler Saw" machines.

All Done with Mirrors

Emile Reynaud (1844–1918) invented the Praxinoscope. This was an improvement on the Magic Lantern and used angled mirrors to project drawings on a moving strip.

Long Exposure
Photography in a camera was invented in France by Joseph-Nicéphore Niepce. In 1816 he captured images using a camera with a lens. The exposure took an entire summer's day.

The Bird Man
Etienne Jules Marey (1830–1894) invented an ingenious rifle-shaped camera to photograph birds in flight . It used a revolving clockwork-powered photographic plate which could take up to 12 pictures a second.

A Penny to See the Peep Show

The first films had an audience of one. They were short peep show attractions shown on the Kinetoscope designed by the American inventor Thomas Alva Edison (1847–1931). The Kinetoscope showed strips of film shot with Edison's Kinetograph, the world's first motion picture camera. Customers dropped a penny into the slot of the box-like Kinetoscope, peered into the stereoscopic viewer and could enjoy a full minute of Buffalo Bill's Wild West show or the quieter pleasures of waves breaking on a beach. The Kinetoscope made Edison a fortune.

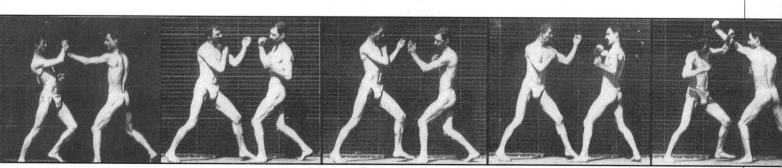

Movies for Money

The Lumière brothers ran a photographic business in France. They were inspired by Edison's Kinetoscope, which they saw in Paris in 1894, but thought its big drawback was that only one person could use it at a time. Louis Lumière designed the Cinematograph, which was a combination of camera and projector, so that films could be shown to a full audience. In Paris on December 28, 1895, Auguste and Louis projected their films to paying customers for the first time.

The First Film Studio

Edison's Kinetoscope shows were filmed with his Kinetograph camera, which was developed in 1888. In 1893 the bulky camera was housed in the world's first purpose-built film studio. The studio was a big windowless box built of tarred paper over a wood frame. Its roof opened to let sunlight in for filming.

Thomas Alva Edison

William Dickson
Dickson was Edison's assistant. He designed the first film studio and directed Edison's very first films. He also experimented with sound films.

Stop That Train!

One of the Lumière brothers' early films showed a train pulling into a station. At the first performance, many of the audience fled in terror, convinced that the train would burst out of the screen into the theatre.

George Eastman
Eastman (1854–1932) developed perforated celluloid film for use in his Kodak box camera. Eastman's film enabled Edison and Dickson to make films in the 35mm gauge (width) which is used for most feature films to this day.

The First Cinemas

A milestone in the development of cinema was the replacement of the nickelodeons by purpose-built movie palaces, the biggest of which could hold up to 5,000 filmgoers, all watching a single screen.

Lost in Space

A space shell scores a direct hit on the Man in the Moon in *A Trip to the Moon*, made in France in 1903 by Georges Méliès. While the Lumières filmed real events in the open air, Méliès was the master of "trick films," which he made in a studio built of glass. Before taking up films, Méliès had been a stage conjuror. In his studio he used special effects photography to create all kinds of illusions on the screen. Many of these effects are still used today. *A Trip to the Moon* was the world's first science fiction epic, lasting all of 21 minutes.

Early Projectors
The first projectors were little more than magic lanterns fitted with a device to advance the film. A crank was turned and a "beater" mechanism advanced the film by dragging on the perforations. This often caused the film to break. As a result early film shows had lots of interruptions.

On Target
When most films lasted only a few minutes, the length of A Trip to the Moon was unusual.

The Movies Are Here to Stay

The French led the way in turning the movies into big business, but the Americans soon overtook them. Most of the early American film-makers worked on the East Coast of the United States, but there were no proper film studios. To catch the sunlight, films were made on the flat roofs of tall buildings. Filming was often interrupted by rain or smoke drifting from neighboring chimneys. In the early 1900s these films—usually only one or two reels long—were shown in halls all over America. The halls were called "nickelodeons" because they charged a nickel (five cents) for admission and, by 1908, there were about 9,000 nickelodeons in America. The Biograph Company was one of the most successful film outfits in the early days of American cinema. Its studio in New York was a training ground for some of the greatest stars of the silent cinema.

STUDIOS AND STARS

The Little Tramp

Charlie Chaplin (1889–1977), pictured below with Jackie Coogan in *The Kid* (1921), was the king of comedy in the silent era. In 1914 he created the Tramp, a lovable outcast, who remains the single most famous character in the history of cinema.

Film Factories

At their peak, each studio had its own style which filmgoers could easily recognize. The biggest and most lavish was MGM (Metro-Goldwyn-Mayer), which boasted that it had "more stars than there are in the heavens." MGM's films were the ultimate in glittering entertainment. In contrast, Warner Brothers was famous for tough social dramas and action-packed gangster movies.

Errol Flynn
In the late 1930s, Errol Flynn was the screen's greatest adventure hero. He was never better than when playing the devil-may-care Robin Hood in The Adventures of Robin Hood *(1938).*

Star Paws
Animals can be stars too. Collie bitch Lassie's first film was in 1943. The original Lassie was actually played by a male dog called Pal. Since then Lassie has always been played by a male dog.

MGM's logo outside a cinema

The Dream Factory

In 1910 the American film industry began to move west to Hollywood, then a sleepy town in California. By 1920, the rapid growth of several big studios meant that Hollywood was producing nearly 800 films a year. For filmgoers, Hollywood meant luxury and glamour, but the reality was very different. The big studios

were highly efficient film factories in which everyone, from the humblest typist to the leading actors and actresses, was an employee. In the early days, film companies did not name the actors who appeared in their films in case they asked for more money. But the public quickly found its favorites and the star system was born.

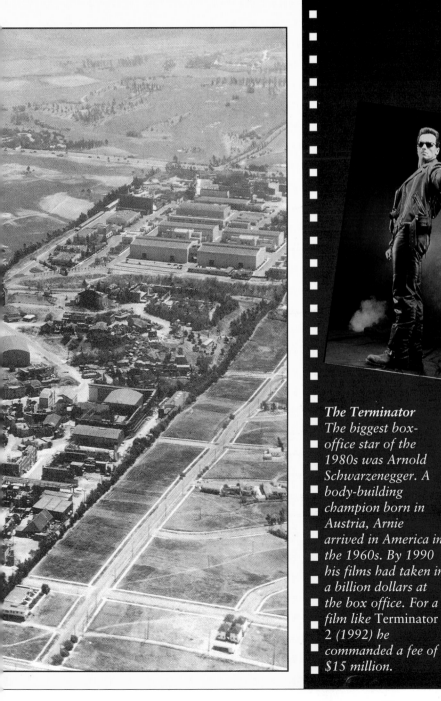

Don't Grow Up! *Macaulay Culkin of* Home Alone *fame is just the latest child star in a line stretching back to the earliest days of cinema. Macaulay has made millions.*

Decline and Fall of Hollywood

Pictured above is a scene from *Time Bandits*, which was produced by Hand Made Films, one of the many independent production companies making films today. Nowadays, independent producers are responsible for many of the films we see, while studios provide the money and the facilities. This trend began in the 1950s when the great days of the Hollywood studios ended. First, television became a serious rival, then film stars began to form their own film companies. More films were made in Europe, where costs were lower than in America, and the studio system broke up, though the studios survived with a variety of new owners.

The Terminator *The biggest box-office star of the 1980s was Arnold Schwarzenegger. A body-building champion born in Austria, Arnie arrived in America in the 1960s. By 1990 his films had taken in a billion dollars at the box office. For a film like* Terminator 2 *(1992) he commanded a fee of $15 million.*

HAND MADE FILMS

THE MOVIE GAME

So you want to be a movie producer? The Movie Game is a simple, snakes-and-ladders version of the real problems, pitfalls and prizes which accompany the production of a big feature film. The movie in this game, a romantic adventure loosely based on the Indiana Jones series, would cost at least $50 million to make. It's a gamble, but everything in the movie business always is. Everyone in Hollywood thinks they know what will be successful, but the truth is, nobody does. You can be a big star one day and an even bigger flop the next. At the beginning of the 1990s no one was bigger than Arnold Schwarzenegger. His films had made profits of over a billion dollars. But in 1993 Arnie made *The Last Action Hero*. The public stayed away and the movie lost its producer, Columbia, over $150 million.

The Movie Game makes another important point. All movies, whether big or small, are the result of a team effort. The film you see on the screen is the result of thousands of decisions made by those involved in its production—creative personnel, craftspeople and technicians as well as the director and stars. Next time you go to a movie watch the credits at the end—they go on forever!

To Play the Game
All you need are dice and some small counters. Take turns to roll the dice and move your counter, following the instructions written on the square you land on.

1 AGENT SEES A NOVEL AND BUYS THE FILM RIGHTS FROM THE AUTHOR AND COMMISSIONS A SCREEN PLAY.

2

3

4 AGENT ASSEMBLES THE STAR AND DIRECTOR GO TO 12

5

6

7 AGENT IS BIG TIME. GO TO 12

8

9 READERS IN THE LITERARY DEPT. READ THE SYNOPSIS. IT IS REJECTED. GO BACK TO 1

10 HEAD OF LITERARY DEPT. LOVES THE SCRIPT. GO TO 12

ENGLAND - SET FILMING
38 FILMING ON SET WITH PRINCIPAL ACTORS.

MACAU - STUNTS AND EXTERIORS
35 FILMING OF EXTERIORS WITH STUNT DOUBLES FOR PRINCIPAL ACTORS.

INDIA - LOCATION SHOOTING
32 FILMING AHEAD OF SCHEDULE. GO TO 35

COLOSSAL PICTURES CORPORATION

12 THE VICE-PRESIDENT IN CHARGE OF MARKETING LIKES THE SCRIPT! GO TO 13

13

14 THE BUDGET FOR FILM PRODUCTION IS TOO HIGH! GO TO 5

11

15

16 BUDGET IS SIGNED BY STUDIO'S DIRECTOR AND THE FILM'S EXECUTIVE PRODUCER.

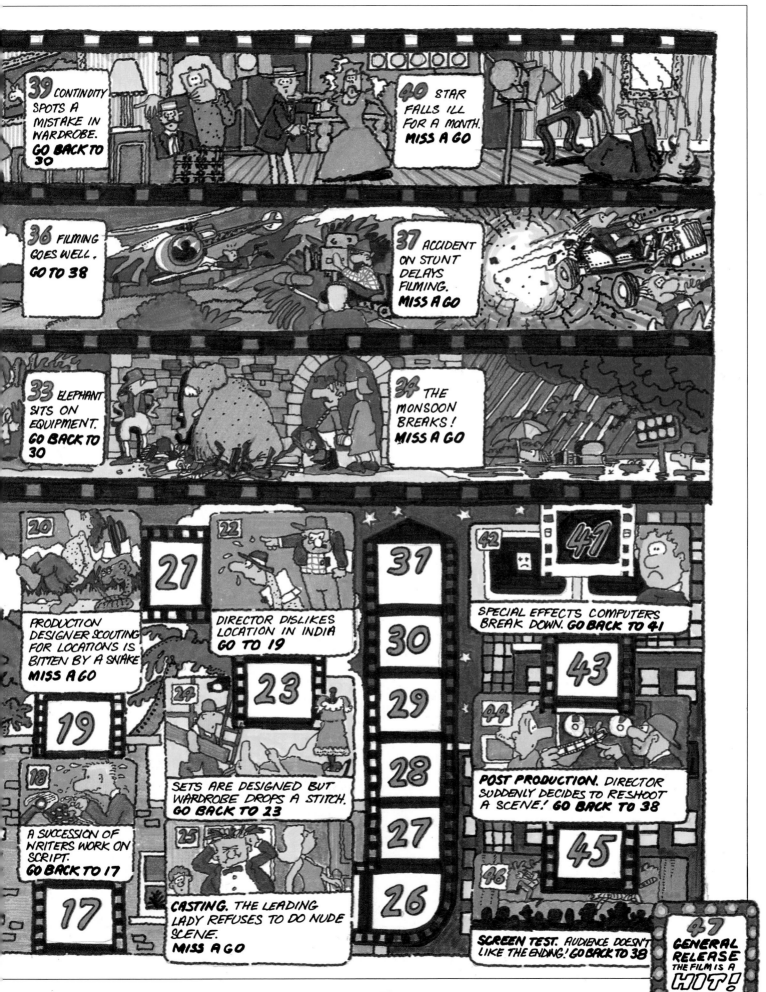

COMEDY AND THRILLERS—
STORYBOARDS, CONTINUITY AND DIRECTING

Thrills and spills have been at the heart of film-making since the cameras began to roll at the turn of the century. In the days of the silent cinema, there was a worldwide language of comedy. Words were not needed to understand the genius of great clowns like Buster Keaton, who is pictured on the left in one of his greatest films, *The General,* which was made in 1927. In films featuring the Keystone Cops, frantic chases were played for laughs. Tastes have changed since those pioneering days, but a sense of timing remains an essential ingredient in both comedies and thrillers. In the best thrillers, the tension is wound up to breaking point before the audience receives a series of carefully planned shocks.

It's All in the Script

There's an old saying in movies that you can't make a good film from a bad screenplay. A screenplay is the written text on which a film is based. But it's never the last word, and is often changed many times during the making of a film. The screenplay for *Total Recall* (1991) was rewritten 50 times!

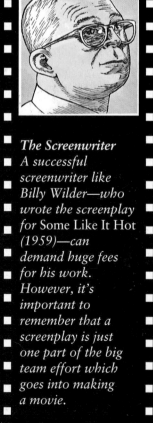

The Screenwriter
A successful screenwriter like Billy Wilder—who wrote the screenplay for Some Like It Hot *(1959)—can demand huge fees for his work. However, it's important to remember that a screenplay is just one part of the big team effort which goes into making a movie.*

Birth of a Film

A movie can spring from a large number of different sources. Producers will pay big money to film best-selling novels or hit plays. Sometimes a news story will inspire a movie—a murder, disaster or scandal taken from the headlines and turned into celluloid. Last but not least are original ideas. They can be very simple: one of the most famous

Harrison Ford in The Fugitive.

Storyboard Artist *Guided by the film's director, the storyboard artist prepares the sketches in great detail because they will be essential reference for the crew and cast.*

is "Arnold Schwarzenegger, Danny de Vito – Twins!", which became a hit film in 1988. In every case the next stage is a brief summary of the play, novel or idea to be shown to a producer. This will give an outline of the story, dramatic highlights and main characters and will only be a few pages long. The next stage is a bigger, more detailed "treatment." Only after the treatment is approved will the first draft of the screenplay be written.

The Storyboard

Most feature films are planned with a storyboard. This is a layout of detailed sketches which outline the flow of action in a movie from start to finish. Some storyboards will also include notes describing the dialogue, music and special effects. Everyone with an important part to play in a movie will be supplied with a copy of the storyboard, and this helps everyone involved in the production of the film to visualize the scenes.

The Director

The director is the man in charge on the movie set. He's the one in the baseball hat bellowing "Action!" when the cameras and sound recorders are ready. But he's involved in a lot more than this. He takes part in the preparation of the shooting script and has a say in the casting of the actors. He will approve the design of the sets and, when shooting is finished, oversee the editing of the film. During filming the director decides where the camera is placed and how the scene will be shot, and also guides the performances of the actors. A genius like Orson Welles (above) wrote, directed and starred in films like *Citizen Kane* (1940), but not every film-maker can keep so many balls in the air at the same time. The most successful director of recent years is Steven Spielberg (right) who has complete control of every aspect of all his films.

Woody Allen
Woody is a leading director of comedies, most of which are set in New York, his hometown.

Casting

Different types of actors are needed in different films, and it's the casting director who selects candidates for a part. They usually have a screen test —a three-minute filmed sequence to see how they look and act on screen. It can be a nerve-racking experience for the actors.

Eye for Detail

Movies are very seldom shot in sequence. Sometimes the last scene is the very first to be filmed, so great care must be taken to match dialogue and details from scene to scene. Everything, including props and backgrounds, must be matched from shot to shot. An actor must not walk into a room wearing a pink shirt and leave in a blue one.

Continuity

A finished film must flow smoothly from start to finish without any jarring breaks or clashes of detail. This is the responsibility of the script supervisor. She stands by the camera during filming, making detailed notes of every scene as it's filmed. At the end of the day these are made up into "continuity sheets," a complete record of the day's work.

Silent Master

Pictured on the left is D.W. Griffith (1875–1948), the most important American director of silent films. His greatest film was Intolerance *(1916).*

Spot the Mistake

See how you would make out as a script supervisor. There are four differences between the two shots shown below. Can you spot them all?

CAMERAS AND CAMERAMEN

In the early 1900s movie cameras were, for the most part, crudely made wooden boxes which had to be cranked by hand. By the 1920s, however, the wooden cameras had been replaced by well-made metal machines like the one in the picture below being used by comedian-director "Fatty" Arbuckle.

The World in Color

Early experiments with color films included coloring each frame of film by hand, an extremely laborious process. The answer was to capture color in the camera. The big breakthrough came in 1932 when the Technicolor Company introduced a camera which used a "three-strip" process to film the colors green, red and blue. The first feature film to be made in three-strip Technicolor was *Becky Sharp* (1935).

How it Works
Film moves though most movie cameras in a stop-start way known as "intermittent." Each frame of film stops for a moment behind a shutter so that it is exposed to the light, and an image is formed through the camera lens. When the shutter closes, a claw moves forward to pull the frame down by its perforations, making room for the next frame. The claw

then pulls back and the shutter opens once again. This process is repeated 24 times every second. Film can also move through a camera by means of a continuous mechanism (shown above). Here the film is driven through the camera by sprocket wheels whose teeth engage the perforations on the film.

The Camera
The basics of the movie camera have changed little since the 1920s. Over 300 yards of film can be stored in a "magazine" on the top and driven through the camera by an electric motor. Since the arrival of sound films in the late 1920s, cameras have been equipped with "blimps," which are soundproof covers designed to muffle the noise of the motor while a film is being shot. The camera's lens is often fitted on a "turret" mount,

Lens
Sophisticated and high-quality lenses are used to capture action.

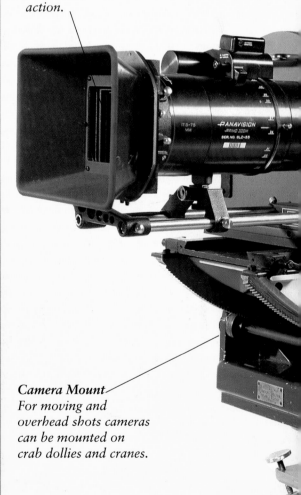

Camera Mount
For moving and overhead shots cameras can be mounted on crab dollies and cranes.

which is a disk on which several lenses can be rotated. Some cameras are equipped with a monitoring viewfinder with a screen on which the image being photographed is reproduced. This is a useful guide for the camera operator in shots when the camera moves.

Film Magazine
The film is stored in these light-proof cases. This allows new film to be loaded quickly and easily.

Viewfinder
Sometimes the camera is attached to a monitor which allows the director to see the action.

Cinematographer
Often called the director of photography, the cinematographer is the chief cameraman. Usually the photography is done by a camera operator working for him.

Focus Puller
This is a member of the camera crew who keeps the lens in focus, particularly during "traveling shots," which require the camera to move.

Clapper Loader
Before a take, the clapper loader snaps the clapper board shut loudly to synchronize sound and vision.

Crab Dolly

A dolly is a wheeled platform on which a camera is mounted for "traveling" shots, usually on the end of a boom, or "arm." The crab dolly's wheels enable it to move like a crab in almost any direction.

The Crane

When the camera swoops down on a scene, it's moving on a long, pivoted boom, mounted on a wheeled trolley. The platform at the end of the boom can seat the director, camera operator and his assistant, and can zoom 6 yards up or down.

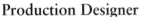
Phantom of the Opera (1925)

HORROR—PRODUCTION DESIGN, MAKE-UP AND LIGHTING

Horror films have been with us a long time, ever since the first vampire movie, *The Haunted Castle*, made in France in 1896. Nearly 100 years later Count Dracula, Frankenstein's monster and a small army of more modern demons are as popular as ever with the public. Horror films play on our deepest fears—of the dark and the unknown—and some of the best horror films have been those in which the monster is never seen but only suggested. Our imaginations do the rest. Nowadays, however, cinemagoers and video buyers have developed a taste for horror movies with ever greater shocks and stunts, in which the blood flows in vast quantities. In these films make-up artists and special effects wizards play a vital part. In recent years, the most popular movie monster has been Freddie Krueger, the taloned terror who first stalked the dreams of terrified teenagers in *A Nightmare on Elm Street* (1985).

Production Designer

More than most films, horror movies depend on atmosphere. This is created by the production designer, who is responsible for the overall "look" of a film, from the set design to its photographic style. All of this must be done within a budget, so the production designer must be a combination of artist and businessman.

Production Designer
He is responsible for the overall "look" of the film.

Haunted Houses

Dianne Wiest (below) wanders through an eerie castle in *Edward Scissorhands* (1991). The production designer was Bo Welch, whose original training as an architect was to prove useful in designing sets. Inset are the members of the *Addams Family* (1991), a comedy-horror movie based on Charles Addams' cartoons in *The New Yorker* magazine.

Boris Karloff
The gaunt Karloff (1887–1969) was an Englishman who leapt to fame in 1931 as the monster in Frankenstein. *His soft, sinister voice was to make him a horror favorite.*

Bela Lugosi
Lugosi (1882–1956) was a Hungarian actor whose chilling tones made him a memorable Count Dracula but typecast him forever.

Lon Chaney, Jr.
The son of a silent star, Chaney (1906–1973) starred as The Wolf Man, The Mummy, Dracula and Frankenstein's monster.

Movie Monsters

Old movie monsters never die. Frankenstein's monster first appeared on screen in a French film of 1906. The monster created from dead bits and pieces later lumbered through other horror films such as *I Was a Teenage Frankenstein* (1957). Bram Stoker's Count Dracula is another durable horror star, appearing as recently as 1992 in *Dracula*. The avenging Mummy was first bandaged up in 1932 and in 1954 co-starred with comics Abbott and Costello in *Abbott and Costello Meet the Mummy*. The Wolf Man has been turning into a raging beast under the full moon since the 1934 *Werewolf of London*, and the Invisible Man first performed his vanishing trick in 1933.

Make-Up Ordeal

In *Frankenstein* (1933) Boris Karloff's monster make-up was devised by Jack Pierce. The box-like head was built up with layers of rubber and cotton. The two metal electrodes on Karloff's neck were fixed so tightly that he had tiny scars there for years afterwards. His face was plastered with blue-green greasepaint, which photographed gray, making him look like a corpse. On his feet were boots normally worn as protective clothing by asphalt spreaders. The total weight of the outfit was nearly 60 lbs. and, with the make-up, took four hours to put on and another two to remove.

Ageing Actors

With the help of a little latex, make-up artistry can turn young actors into senior citizens. In *Little Big Man* (1970), 33-year-old Dustin Hoffman played two scenes as a 121-year-old survivor of the Wild West. Make-up artist Dick Smith cast a mold of Hoffman's head and shoulders and then worked for three months to make a foam latex mask for the actor to age him 88 years!

Man into Monster
Fredric March turns from Dr. Jekyll to Mr. Hyde in 1932. Though the transformation flows smoothly before our eyes, it was achieved by using filters removed one by one to reveal make-up changes and by stopping the camera on held poses to apply make-up on set.

Freddy's Face

Taloned terror Freddy Krueger strikes a thoughtful pose (below), possibly pondering on how he got that frightful face. The make-up for the star of the *Nightmare on Elm Street* movies, played by Robert Englund, was created by make-up wizard David Miller. The secret was a specially created foam latex mask which took up to four hours to apply. To make the mask, foam latex was whipped up in a blender. After letting it rise, it was injected into a mold which was then baked for four hours. The molded rubber mask which emerged did not reflect light

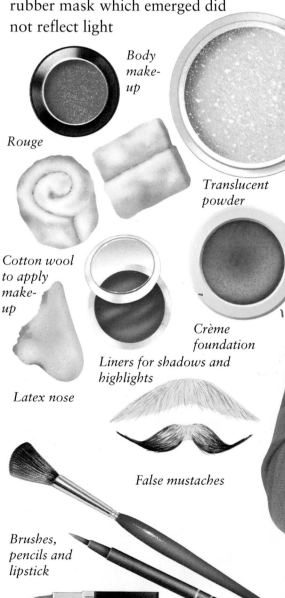

Body make-up

Rouge

Translucent powder

Cotton wool to apply make-up

Crème foundation

Liners for shadows and highlights

Latex nose

False mustaches

Brushes, pencils and lipstick

like human skin, so the lights on the set had to be toned down during filming. The mask was put on in three stages. First pre-prepared rubber appliances were fixed to Englund's face. Then a head cap was fitted and ears attached. Glue held everything together while make-up blended the separate parts together. Englund's make-up would stay on his face for most of a gruelling 14-hour day in the studio.

False ear

Make-up Artist
Film star Marlene Dietrich said that actors and make-up artists were partners in crime. The crime is transforming often quite ordinary-looking actors into figures of glamour or terror. Sometimes the dividing line between make-up and special effects is very thin.

False eyelashes

Stipple sponge used for ageing make-up

An American Werewolf in London (1981). In the transformation scene the werewolf's expanding hands (below) were not the actor's but dummy hands covered with a special putty called "smooth-on." Hidden syringes pumped air into the hands to make them swell.

Blood and Gore
In the zombie epic *Dawn of the Dead* (1979) make-up man Tom Savini created a special effect to make a man's head explode. A dummy was constructed topped by a lifelike head with a latex skin. Inside the head were a dozen fake blood sacs and such odd items as apple cores and corn chips. The head was then blown off with a shotgun.

Spirit gum to glue hair and liquid latex to create scars.

Lighting

The look and feel of a film depend on the lighting used in the production. The cinematographer—the person in charge of lighting the set and photographing the film—is responsible for creating the mood required by the director. Lighting is just as important outdoors on location as it is in the studio. Natural light can be increased by extra lights or reflectors, which can be used to light dark corners or highlight faces. On location the lights are the heaviest items of equipment. The top-heavy arc lamps, known as "brutes," are used to simulate sunlight and are vital in color filming. Flood lamps and spot lamps of different sizes, shapes and strengths are also used. The main source of illumination is the "key light" from the arc lamps.

Klaus Kinski
Kinski (1926–1991)
was a German film
star often cast in
sinister roles like the
evil vampire in
Nosferatu (1979).

Moment of Terror

A monster appears in *Dracula* (1992). The film is a feast of special effects created "in the camera." For an effect known as "pixilation"—in which actors move about in a strange, jerky way—the director, Francis Ford Coppola, used an old hand-cranked camera from the days of silent cinema. Some scenes were shot in reverse, with actors moving backwards, to give an eerie effect when the film was re-run forward.

Reflector

Black screen (gobo)

Series of lights
with a diffuser

Arc lights with
barn doors

Smoke Gets in Your Eyes

In the past smoke and fog effects were often produced by burning kerosene or pouring water over dry ice. Now banks of fog can be called up at the push of a button from a number of portable devices.

Portable smoke machine

Wet and Windy

A wind machine is just a large fan which can brush actors with a summer breeze or lash them with hurricane force. Sometimes it joins forces with a wind howler to produce the noise of a howling gale. In the studio or on location, rain falls with the help of hoses, perforated pipes and sprinkler systems. A "rain standard" is often used to produce a shower. This is a sprinkler on a mobile tripod which hangs about 9 yards above the actors' heads. Bigger storms are created with a system of sprinklers known as a "rain cluster." To complete the illusion puddles are spread about before shooting and slick surfaces painted on walls.

Sprinkler

The Gaffer
The chief electrician on a film unit, the "gaffer," is in charge of lighting the set. He oversees the positioning of the lights before shooting begins.

Dracula appears in a hideous form in an atmospheric sequence in the film Dracula *(1992).*

Supernatural Storm

The sprinklers and wind machine are working overtime as Heather O'Rourke hits a spot of supernatural trouble in *Poltergeist* (1982).

WAR AND WESTERNS—
LOCATION SHOOTING, PROPS AND EXTRAS

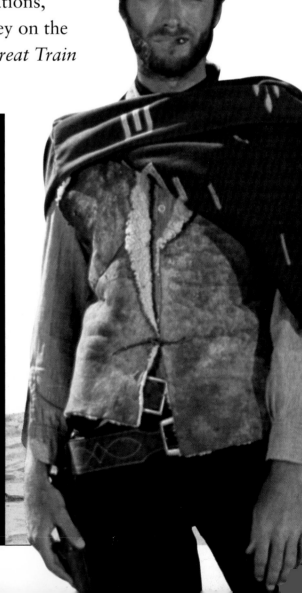

War films and Westerns have been popular film fare for at least ninety years, satisfying our craving for action and adventure. Since the turn of the century well over 7,000 Westerns have been made and, though they began in America, they were later made all over the world. The landscape of the Western is instantly recognizable from Pittsburgh to Peking: cowboys and Indians, wagon trains, riding off into the sunset. In 1894 the real-life Western heroine Annie Oakley appeared in a short film. But the first motion picture to tell a story with a Western setting was probably *The Great Train Robbery* (1903). Although it had genuine outdoor locations, they were not filmed in the Wild West but in New Jersey on the East Coast of America. In the scene above from *The Great Train Robbery*, an outlaw fires at the audience.

The Big Country

Dramatic outdoor settings are the trademark of the Western. In the early years of films the search for genuine Western scenery led many film companies to California, where sunny skies and and sweeping landscapes provided the perfect backdrop for fast and furious Western action. Perhaps the most famous location is Monument Valley in Utah. It was used many times by the great Western director John Ford.

Location Spotting
Before filming begins, the right locations are scouted. A broad selection of locations is usually whittled down until a final choice is made by the director and production designer. Finding the right location for a period film can be difficult.

The Man with No Name
Clint Eastwood (left) starred as the mysterious gunfighter in *For a Few Dollars More* (1965). This was one of a number of successful roles for Eastwood in films that became known as "Spaghetti Westerns" because they had Italian directors. The films were shot in southern Spain, because the landscape there looks very like the American West.

Images of War
A dramatic scene from the Vietnam war epic Apocalypse Now *(1979), directed by Francis Ford Coppola.*

Big John
John Wayne (1907–1979) was the biggest Western star of them all. In nearly 90 screen appearances as a cowboy, he only bit the dust four times.

Action Stations
The easiest way to survive an Indian attack is in the studio. Here our cowboy hero rides a dummy horse while a wind machine and back-projected film of landscape racing past complete the illusion.

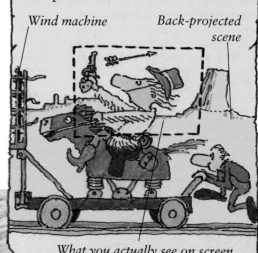

Wind machine   *Back-projected scene*

What you actually see on screen

Props

"Props" is short for properties. These the furniture, fixtures, decorations and moveable items of all kinds which are seen or used on the film set but are not part of the set's structure. Each studio has a prop department which stores and catalogs a fantastic variety of props from simple items like swords and rifles to huge and elaborate items of machinery built specially for a movie. A prop man might be called on to supply anything, from a sandwich to a siege engine. The arrangement of props on the set is done by a set decorator. His work is then checked by the property master to ensure that all the props needed for the scene are present and correct.

Prop Master
The prop master finds all the items required by the set designer. Sometimes they are specially made, but he will often go out and buy them himself.

David Niven
David Niven's road to stardom began in 1934 when he signed on in Hollywood as a film extra.

Big Flop

One of the biggest financial disasters in Hollywood history was a hugely expensive Western, *Heaven's Gate* (1980). It was originally planned to cost about $12 million dollars but the final bill came to $40 million, mainly because of lavish sets (right) and director Michael Cimino's obsession with detail. The loss the film made ruined the movie's backer, United Artists, which was then taken over by MGM.

Duel for the Sky

Aerial combat is very hard to film but, at its best, it can be very exciting, as in *The Blue Max* (1966). From the ground, a dogfight looks a bit like two flies chasing each other—the most spectacular results are achieved when stunt fliers and cameramen specializing in aerial photography take to the skies. Dramatic close-ups can then be added in the studio.

Stills Photographer
He's the snapper on the set, taking pictures as a record of the production and to publicize the movie.

Superstars
Robert Redford (top) and Paul Newman, who formed a hugely successful partnership playing outlaws in Butch Cassidy and the Sundance Kid *(1968) and con-men in* The Sting *(1973).*

Keep 'em Flying
The cast of the World War II film Memphis Belle *(1991) poses in front of the vintage B-17 bomber used in the movie. These veteran warplanes are in great demand for movies.*

Bloody Ending

A Western villain is shot with the help of a special effects compressed-air gun. It fires soft gelatin pellets filled with "blood" that burst dramatically when they hit their target.

What you actually see on screen

Compressed air

Air gun

A highly authentic scene from Heaven's Gate *shows a steam train in action during the early pioneering days.*

Extras

Extras are non-speaking members of the cast who are used to fill in the background to a film or to form a crowd. In America they are supplied according to type and number required by the Central Casting Corporation, which was set up in 1926. Some extras specialize in certain roles and have their own costumes. In *The Ten Commandments* (1956) director Cecil B. De Mille used 12,000 extras!

Coordinator
The job of the co-ordinator is to make sure that everything runs smoothly on location.

Star Treatment

Movie stars seldom rough it on location. They can relax in air-conditioned mobile homes with every modern convenience.

Last of the Mohicans

Daniel Day-Lewis (above) starred as the white man raised by Indians in *The Last of the Mohicans* (1992). The movie was filmed in North Carolina and all the extras were Native Americans. To prepare for the role, Day-Lewis went on a woodlands survival and weapons training course and ran for miles with a musket on his back.

Daniel Day-Lewis
A versatile young film actor, Day-Lewis immerses himself completely in each of his roles.

On the Road

Filming outside the studio on location is like moving a small army around. A convoy of heavy transporters carries the lights, generators and all the equipment needed for filming. Buses bring in the actors and extras.

On Location

Food and hotel bills for the cast and crew on location can eat up a sizeable part of a movie's budget. The canteen compensates for the

Extra, Extra!
In The Battle of Waterloo *(1970) the thousands of extras were Russian soldiers.*

discomfort and boredom of shooting on location by providing vast amounts of good food.

STUNT ARTISTS

Engulfed in flames in films like *Robocop 2* (1990), stunt men and women live dangerously. They stand in for the actors when there's a risk to life and limb and, in the past, took terrible risks. Now they are well-organized professionals who plan every stunt with great care. Movies with a stunting background include *Hooper* (1978) and *The Stunt Man* (1980).

The unstoppable lawman in Robocop *(1987)*

Yakima Canutt
The greatest of all stunt men, Yakima Canutt (1895–1986) is best known for his work on Stagecoach *(1939) and as director of the chariot race in* Ben Hur *(1959). He was originally a rodeo rider and star of silent Westerns. In* The Devil Horse *(1931), his stunts included a 27-yard clifftop leap on horseback.*
The Last Action Hero (1993)

The Kicker Ramp

A stunt man flies through the air with the greatest of ease with the aid of a hinged kicker ramp. Compressed air flips him up to 3 yards onto a crash mat.

Playing with Fire

Fire sequences are dangerous and always very carefully planned, using fuel that burns at low temperatures. It burns yellow and orange with lots of smoke so that it can actually be picked up by the camera and make the shot more spectacular.

Flameproof under-hood

Flameproof undergarment

Lifelike mask and hands

Protective suits and goggles are worn in fire scenes and a mask of the actor for whom the stunt artist is doubling is worn over the goggles. Fire-resistant polymer gels can protect ordinary clothes for up to 30 seconds, although shots rarely last longer than 15.

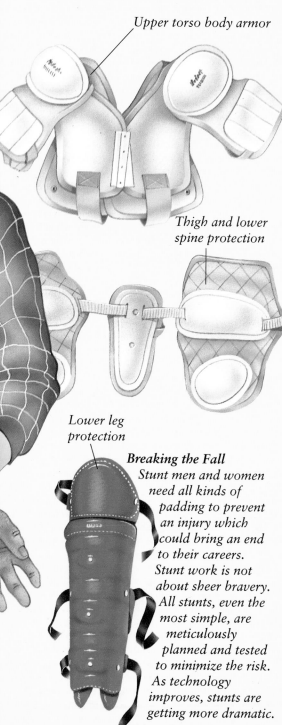

Upper torso body armor

Thigh and lower spine protection

Lower leg protection

Breaking the Fall
Stunt men and women need all kinds of padding to prevent an injury which could bring an end to their careers. Stunt work is not about sheer bravery. All stunts, even the most simple, are meticulously planned and tested to minimize the risk. As technology improves, stunts are getting more dramatic.

Breakaways
These are props or part of a set specially made with lightweight materials so that they will easily shatter or fall apart during an action sequence or a big fight scene.

The Stunt Man
Some stunt artists specialize in particular skills such as underwater work or car crashes. But they all need to be fit and to possess a broad range of abilities, including riding, a knowledge of the martial arts and free-fall parachuting. In big films with lots of stunts the work of a number of stunt artists is organized by a stunt co-ordinator. In the disaster movie The Towering Inferno *(1974) there were no fewer than 140 stunt artists.*

Man on a Wire
Stunt artists are always devising new ways to thrill. Stunt man Vic Armstrong's fan descender can drop people from a great height without having them free-fall. They are actually held in a harness on the end of a wire wrapped around a rotating spool. The spool drives a spinning fan and the air resistance on the fan slows the speed at which the wire runs out. In *The Last Action Hero* (1992) Arnold Schwarzenegger's stunt double Peter Kent used the fan descender to fall over 30 yards.

Wild Wheels
A concealed ramp can flip the largest of vehicles over. Sometimes car crashes use air cannons built into the underside of the car. Then a charge of compressed air blasts a ram out of the cannon and pushes the car to make it roll.

Historical Epics—
Glass painting, wardrobe and sets

Spectacular historical epics are as old as cinema itself. In 1912 the Italians made an eight-reel version of *Quo Vadis* which was set in Ancient Rome. It boasted colossal sets, thousands of extras and real lions. American director D. W. Griffith was so impressed that he immediately started making epics of his own. They bankrupted him, and the cost of epic films has escalated to cause film-makers problems ever since. In 1927 MGM nearly went bust after spending almost $5 million on another Roman spectacular, *Ben Hur*. At the time it was the most expensive film ever made. In 1959 MGM spent over $14 million on a remake, but this time it made a big profit and won 11 Oscars.

Getting It Wrong

Historical films do not always paint an accurate picture of the past. Mistakes sometimes creep in. In one scene in *Camelot* (1967), a musical about King Arthur and the Knights of the Round Table, King Arthur (played by Richard Harris) has a Band-Aid on his neck! In *The Viking Queen* (1966), a movie set in Roman Britain, one of the actors can be spotted wearing a wristwatch!

Gone With the Wind

The most successful movie of all time, *Gone With the Wind* (or *GWTW* as movie people call it), was adapted from Margaret Mitchell's best-selling novel of the American Civil War. Many hands were involved in the production, including four different directors and 15 screenwriters. Producer David O. Selznick wrote much of the script himself and even directed some of the scenes. *GWTW* had a spectacular première in Atlanta on December 15, 1939.

The Grip
The grip is a jack of all trades. On the film set he operates much like a stagehand in the theatre. He moves props from scene to scene, builds platforms and other structures, lays tracks for the camera on location and puts camera and sound recording equipment in place.

Rhett and Scarlett
Clark Gable and Vivien Leigh starred in GWTW as Rhett Butler and Scarlett O'Hara. Rhett's last words to Scarlett, "Frankly, my dear, I don't give a damn," caused a sensation at the time as swearing in movies was strictly forbidden.

Castles in the Air

How do you put a castle in a movie without building it? In fact, all you need is a sheet of glass. The castle is painted onto the glass, which is then placed in front of the camera to form part of the background to the live action.

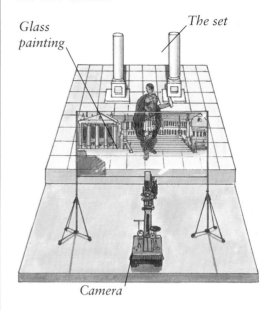

Glass painting

The set

Camera

Hanging Miniatures

This trick involves carefully placing a small-scale model in front of the camera so that it blends with the background. For Rome's Circus Maximus in the 1927 version of *Ben Hur*, a stadium was made that had a real bottom half with real people as spectators. But the upper section was a hanging miniature with 10,000 mechanical figures that could stand up and wave.

What you see on the screen

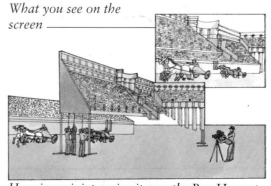

Hanging miniature in situ on the Ben Hur *set*

Dressing Up

Costumes in films can range from Tarzan's simple loincloth to the dazzling, historically accurate clothes worn in films like *Orlando* (1993). Today, costume designers and makers never know what they might have to create next, but in the early years of cinema actors wore their own clothes or hired costumes from theatrical prop companies. The story goes that in 1914 Charlie Chaplin created the costume of the Tramp by borrowing items of clothing belonging to fellow comedians at the Keystone studio. In the 1920s, however, the big studios built up their own costume departments. They became Aladdin's

Hat Trick
Elizabeth Taylor in the title role of Cleopatra (1963), *a ruinously expensive epic, wore a crown of pure gold. It cost $6,500, but this was a fraction of the cost of her life-size royal barge—a staggering $250,000.*

caves which producers could plunder for films with historical or modern settings. When the talkies arrived at the end of the 1920s, costumes suddenly posed unexpected problems. The crude microphones of the day picked up every rustle, forcing costume designers to seek out softer, silent fabrics. In the heyday of the big Hollywood studios, costumes in historical films were often more extravagant than they were accurate. The emphasis was on creating the right atmosphere for the film rather

Elizabeth Taylor and Richard Burton in Cleopatra.

than paying attention to period detail. Nowadays great care is taken to create costumes which are convincing copies of the clothes people wore in the past. Costume designers study paintings and books relating to the period. Historical costumes are hand-stitched as the stitches made by sewing machines look too neat and modern.

A glittering example of the costume designers' art from Excalibur.

Batman's Costume

Costume designer Ron Ringword made the Batsuit worn by Michael Keaton in *Batman* (1989). A glass fiber replica of the actor was used as a mold for the muscled outer suit, which was then sculpted in clay and cast in foam rubber sections. The sections were attached to a cotton-lycra body suit with a rubberized surface, made shiny with silicone. Over 20 Batsuits were made for Keaton and his stunt doubles.

Costume Designer
After studying the script, the period and the setting, the costume designer prepares color sketches for the approval of the director and production designer before producing the final designs. The most famous costume designer is Edith Head, winner of many Academy Awards.

A Stitch in Time

While the stars and principal actors, like Kenneth Branagh in *Henry V* (1989) (below), have their clothes specially made for them, actors with smaller parts are dressed by costume hire companies. On their racks hang thousands of costumes of all kinds. During filming the costumes are taken care of by a man or woman known as the wardrobe master or mistress. As a group, these important members of the crew are known as costumers. Several weeks before the shooting of a film begins, a team of costumers (usually about four) joins the production. After looking closely at the script they collect items of costume from the studio wardrobe or rental companies. When filming begins, the costumers oversee the fitting of the less important actors and extras. They also help the stars to dress before the cameras roll. In historical films and Westerns a lot of work goes into "distressing" costumes—making them look old, muddy or dirty.

Historical detail is important to make films like Henry V *believable.*

Illusions of Grandeur

No self-respecting epic is complete without a cast of thousands milling around a monster set. The biggest single set ever built for a motion picture was for *The Fall of the Roman Empire* (1964), which was shot in Spain. It was a replica of the Forum, the hub of Ancient Rome. The set stood on a 200,000-square-yard site outside Madrid. It measured 400 by 226 yards and rose to a height of 78 yards. It included 27 full-size buildings, 601 marble columns and 350 statues. The cost of this huge folly bankrupted the movie's producer, Samuel Bronston, but not before he had gone on to sink a real and very large ship in another spectacular movie, *Circus World* (1964).

Warrior Hero
For many years Charlton Heston was Hollywood's favorite epic hero. He played Moses in The Ten Commandments *(1956) and the medieval Spanish hero El Cid in 1961, and he won a Best Actor Oscar playing the title role in* Ben Hur *in 1959, the pinnacle of his film career.*

Ancient City

It took the great American director D. W. Griffith two years and $2.5 million to make *Intolerance* (1916). Part of the film was set in Babylon, for which Griffith built a set covering 40,470 square yards. The life-size replica of the city had massive 30-yard walls, even taller towers, and eight immense columns topped by statues of rearing elephants.

In the Studio

Interior scenes are usually shot on a sound stage—a soundproof studio underneath a complete lighting rig. Sometimes whole films are made in the studio with no outside location work, such as *One from the Heart* (1982), in which the city of Las Vegas was created inside the studio.

The Model Maker *Computer effects still cannot produce anything as detailed as the work of a model maker.*

Models

Models play an important part in the planning of a movie. Scale replicas of the sets help the director of photography to work out the lighting and where to place a crane or dolly tracks for a difficult shot.

A typical example of a sound stage shows the facade of the buildings hiding the skeleton construction behind.

Up in Flames

How did they re-create the burning of Atlanta in the American Civil War epic *Gone With the Wind* (1939)? It was actually one of the huge sets from *King Kong* filmed six years earlier that was burned down—making one of the most spectacular blazes ever filmed.

Carpenters

The craftspeople who build movie sets usually work in relays so that they do not get in each other's way as the set rises around them. First the carpenters erect the walls, which are then painted or papered. They return to fix the moldings and, after those have been painted, they hang the doors and fit windows.

TAKE 4 THE BIG SCREEN

The standard movie gauge (width) is 35mm. Sometimes 35mm is enlarged to make a print on 70mm for showing in big cinemas. Vistavision and CinemaScope are special screen formats for wider screens, but are not in general use now. Vistavision was revived by George Lucas in 1977 for *Star Wars*. Home movies are shot in 16mm, 8mm or Super 8.

1. 70mm
2. 35mm
3. CinemaScope
4. Vistavision
5. 16mm

CinemaScope

A wide-screen process of the 1950s, the CinemaScope camera, uses a special lens to "squeeze" a wide picture onto a standard 35mm frame which is then projected through a similar lens.

Abel Gance
A French film director, Gance (1889–1981) was a pioneer of wide-screen techniques. His work is often revived.

Triple Screen
Parts of Abel Gance's spectacular Napoléon (1927) were shot by three synchronized cameras and shown on a wide triple screen. The result looked forward to the Cinerama wide-screen process of the 1950s.

This Gaumont Kalee projector was used in the 1950s. A projector is simply a device for throwing images onto a screen. When a succession of images is projected at the right speed, the illusion of motion pictures is created.

Lamp House
Powerful arc lamps provide the light for the projector.

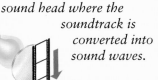

Moving Pictures
In the projector each frame of film is guided into position by pins or claws which hold it for a moment in a beam of light in the picture gate. This throws the image onto the screen; the film travels on through the sound head where the soundtrack is converted into sound waves.

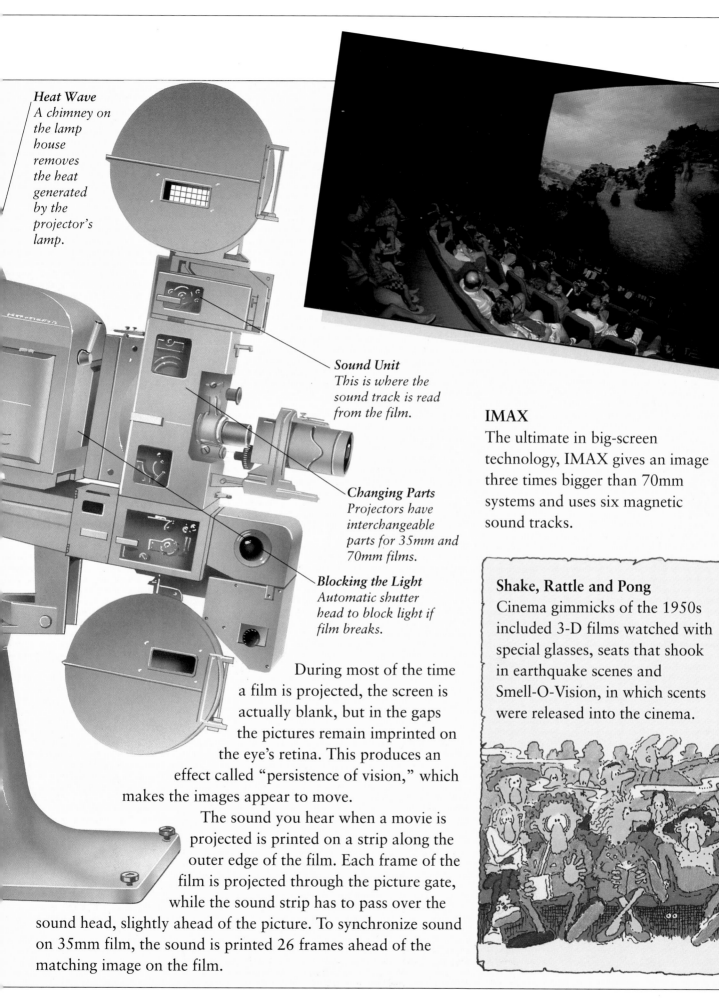

Heat Wave
A chimney on the lamp house removes the heat generated by the projector's lamp.

Sound Unit
This is where the sound track is read from the film.

Changing Parts
Projectors have interchangeable parts for 35mm and 70mm films.

Blocking the Light
Automatic shutter head to block light if film breaks.

IMAX

The ultimate in big-screen technology, IMAX gives an image three times bigger than 70mm systems and uses six magnetic sound tracks.

During most of the time a film is projected, the screen is actually blank, but in the gaps the pictures remain imprinted on the eye's retina. This produces an effect called "persistence of vision," which makes the images appear to move.

The sound you hear when a movie is projected is printed on a strip along the outer edge of the film. Each frame of the film is projected through the picture gate, while the sound strip has to pass over the sound head, slightly ahead of the picture. To synchronize sound on 35mm film, the sound is printed 26 frames ahead of the matching image on the film.

Shake, Rattle and Pong

Cinema gimmicks of the 1950s included 3-D films watched with special glasses, seats that shook in earthquake scenes and Smell-O-Vision, in which scents were released into the cinema.

MUSICALS—SOUND AND SOUND EFFECTS

The film musical was the only new type of movie to be born at the end of the 1920s when the talkies arrived. Silent movies were never, in fact, completely silent. In big cinemas a full-scale orchestra could often accompany films, and even in the smallest "fleapit" a piano pounded away. There were also experiments with sound. Most of them involved attempting to synchronize the film with a sound track on a gramophone disk, but these systems were always breaking down. The only answer was to record sound onto the film next to the picture. The resulting sound track has brought us such musical gems as *Singin' in the Rain* (1952), starring Gene Kelly.

Off to See the Wizard

Judy Garland and friends appeared in *The Wizard of Oz* (1939), the most delightful fantasy musical ever made. The film's most famous song is "Over the Rainbow," which won an Oscar and is as fresh today as when Judy first sang it.

Busby Berkeley
Musical director Berkeley (1895–1976) specialized in kaleidoscopic dance routines packed with dozens of glamorous girls.

The Jazz Singer

In 1927 the Warner Brothers studio was on the point of going broke. They sank everything into *The Jazz Singer*, starring Al Jolson (above). It was a partly silent movie with some clumsily synchronized musical and speaking sequences. In one of these Jolson uttered the immortal words, "You ain't heard nothin' yet!" Within a year silent cinema was a

Sound Track

If you hold the emulsion side of a strip of film toward you, you will see the sound track in a narrow band on the left side of the frame. The sound track is made up of four parts which carry the movie's dialogue, music and sound effects plus a reserve track.

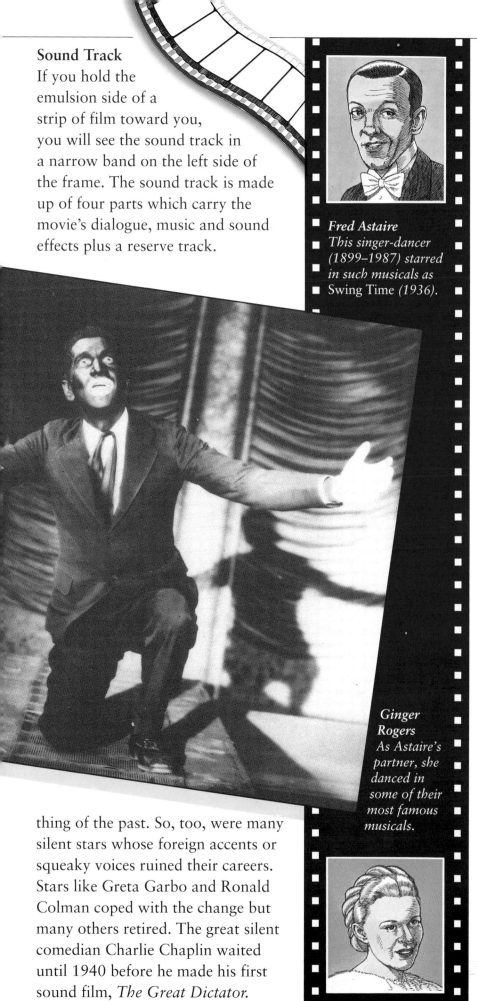

thing of the past. So, too, were many silent stars whose foreign accents or squeaky voices ruined their careers. Stars like Greta Garbo and Ronald Colman coped with the change but many others retired. The great silent comedian Charlie Chaplin waited until 1940 before he made his first sound film, *The Great Dictator.*

Fred Astaire
This singer-dancer (1899–1987) starred in such musicals as Swing Time (1936).

Ginger Rogers
As Astaire's partner, she danced in some of their most famous musicals.

Foreign Editions

In the early days of the talkies Hollywood films were made in several foreign language versions, each with a different cast. This expensive and time-consuming business was eventually replaced by dubbing.

Vitaphone

The Vitaphone system used for the sound sequences in *The Jazz Singer* was a sound-on-disc process which was soon overtaken by the superior sound-on-film method. Vitaphone was abandoned in 1931.

Movie Music

After a film has been edited, each scene is timed and the music composed and played to fit what is happening on the screen. The composer will have sketched in the musical themes earlier on.

Sound Mixers

Sound mixers work in a recording studio to combine all the recorded sound tracks into a single sound track. This composite track will go on the print released to cinemas.

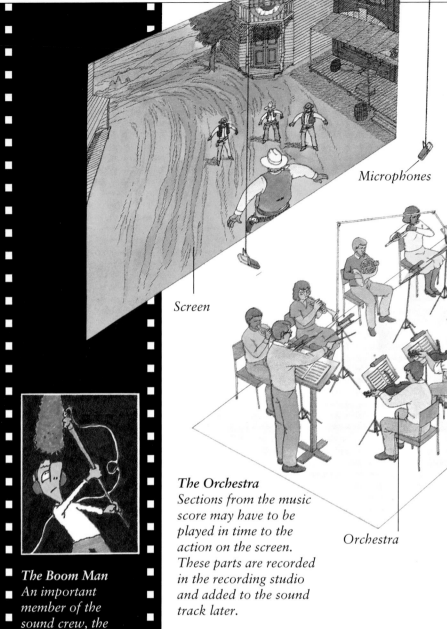

Microphones

Screen

The Orchestra
Sections from the music score may have to be played in time to the action on the screen. These parts are recorded in the recording studio and added to the sound track later.

Orchestra

The Boom Man
An important member of the sound crew, the boom maneuvers the microphone during filming on the end of a long, moveable arm.

Theme Music

To create a film's music track, the orchestra works in a scoring studio, a sound stage equipped with a screen. The film is run, the orchestra plays in time with the action and the score is recorded. The composer is an important member of a movie's creative team, and music is a powerful ingredient in establishing atmosphere. It's impossible to think of *Jaws* (1975), for example, without recalling the powerful theme written for the movie by John Williams. It matched perfectly the image of a

Music to Match
A projector runs the film while the orchestra plays the timed score. A single music track can also be mixed from musicians playing separately. The first film to have a synchronized musical score was Fritz Lang's epic Siegfried, *made in Germany in 1925.*

André Previn
One of the best-known composers of film scores, André Previn has won three Oscars since starting to write for films in 1949.

A New Voice
Dubbing means adding sound (effects, music, song, dialogue) to pictures already shot. It can also mean replacing the film's dialogue with a new version in a foreign language.

Recording studio

huge shark, that no one could see, churning through the water toward its prey.

Many Sounds
All the many recordings are played together on one multitape recorder to create the final film sound track.

Make Your Own Sound Effects
Sound engineering in the movies employs a battery of hi-tech equipment, but with a tape recorder you can make your own simple sound effects. Try using different types of surfaces for footsteps, and coconuts for horses' hooves. And, for your first horror movie, a cabbage and a saw will simulate the gruesome sound of a limb being sawn off by a mad professor.

SCIENCE FICTION—
MODEL MAKING, SPECIAL EFFECTS AND ANIMATRONICS

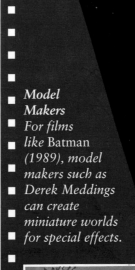

Step into our Time Machine and travel back to the days of the very first science fiction movie, *The Mechanical Butcher* (1895), in which a live pig is squeezed into a large box and emerges at the other end conveniently converted into an array of bacon, sausages and spare ribs. Ever since its early days science fiction cinema has used trick photography and special effects to transport us to other worlds and to ask the simple question "What if?" In the past, science fiction films were not taken very seriously. One exception was Fritz Lang's brilliant silent film *Metropolis* (1927) (above), set in a vast city of the future. But science fiction films have struck back. The two biggest money-earners of all time are science fiction films produced and directed by Steven Spielberg—*Jurassic Park* (1993) and *E.T.* (1982).

Models

Lots of special effects are created by using models of varying sizes. For *Superman* the special effects crew built an 18-yard-high replica of the Boulder Dam. The crystalline surface of the ice-planet Krypton was a plaster and fiberglass construction that filled an entire sound stage.

Model Makers
For films like Batman *(1989), model makers such as Derek Meddings can create miniature worlds for special effects.*

Traveling Matte

A spaceship shoots across the screen with the aid of a "traveling matte." This is a way of combining moving actors or miniatures with a pre-filmed background. The spaceship is fitted into the scene by creating an exactly matching hole in the background. This

involves something called a "blue-screen process," which is shown above. In Step 1, the background of the planet is shot. In Step 2, the spaceship is filmed against a blue background which does not register on color film. From this shot a matte is prepared consisting of a black silhouette of the ship against a clear background (Step 3 and 4). When the matte is printed together with the shot of the planet (Step 5), it leaves a hole with the shape of the ship in it. Another matte, this time blocking out the blue background, is then printed together with the original shot of the spaceship. In the last stage (Step 6) the image of the spaceship is printed into the "hole." The work of combining these shots is done in a gadget called an optical printer.

The spaceships vary in size to help overcome scale on long-distance shots.

Star Wars

Many of the best effects in *Star Wars* (1977) relied on traditional methods—make-up, backdrop paintings and models. It's done so skillfully that it's impossible to spot where real people and full-size sets take over from the models.

Harrison Ford
Ford achieved fame playing Hans Solo in Star Wars.

Flying Tonight

The blue-screen process is only one of the ways in which an actor can "fly." In *Batman* (1989) the Caped Crusader's leaps were accomplished using wires. Another way of getting actors airborne is front projection. The 1970s saw a revolution in special effects that began with *Star Wars*. The film's director, George Lucas, built up a brilliant young effects team to bring his vision of the battle between Empire and Rebels

Front Projection

The background is projected on to a screen off a two-way mirror placed at a 45-degree angle. The screen reflects the image back through the mirror to the camera. Lights wash out any of the projected image which falls on the actor or set. Superman flies!

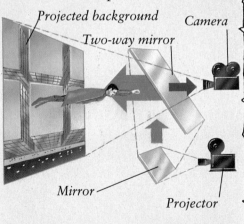

Projected background

Camera

Two-way mirror

Mirror

Projector

The finished scene

Daring Deeds
Superman flies in front of a front projection, while Harrison Ford clings to a ledge above a matte.

Hanging On

Live-action footage of the exciting rooftop climax in *Blade Runner* (1982) was combined with a matte painting to leave dogged detective Harrison Ford hanging by his fingernails over a dizzying drop.

to the big screen. The team later formed Industrial Light and Magic (ILM), the world's leading special effects company. ILM used many traditional techniques in *Star Wars,* but they also developed new ones using computers for the first time in special effects. They pioneered a system called "motion control" in which cameras are fixed to programmed mountings that can then move in complex patterns, filming all the time. The light-sabers wielded by Luke Skywalker and Darth Vader evolved gradually. At first they tried real glowing sticks. Then the sticks were "rotoscoped," using a simple animation process. By the time ILM came to create the effects in *Return of the Jedi* (1983), the last of the Star Wars films, they were using computer animation for the light-sabers.

Keaton and Pfeiffer
Michael Keaton (above) starred as the Caped Crusader in Batman *(1989) and* Batman Returns *(1992). In* Batman Returns, *he was joined by Michelle Pfeiffer, who played Batman's slinky enemy, Cat Woman.*

Batman

In *Batman* (1989) most of Gotham City was created by using so-called "miniatures," though some of them were as high as 9 yards. The power station which blows up in one scene is a 2-yard miniature built like a jigsaw to explode predictably. Parts of this sequence were also shot in a real disused power station outside London. It was set alight in controlled conditions using liquid gas pumped through 600 yards of piping. There were several models of the Batwing: tiny 6-inch toys, a 3-yard model with a radio-controlled Batman puppet inside, and a life-size model of Batman's shot-down plane.

Racing Chassis
The Batmobile was a Chevrolet chassis wrapped in streamlined kevlar, used on racing cars.

The Dark Crystal
This fantasy about a couple of elf-like creatures on a quest featured many animatronic puppets as well as traditionally operated puppets.

Animatronics

Stop-frame animation is not the only way to move creature models around. Some, like the Teenage Mutant Ninja Turtles on the right, are operated by an actor and filmed normally. The actor, sweating inside the costume, controls the model's movements though not its facial expressions. This is done by a puppeteer who uses cable or radio control to move the mouth and other features. This technique, dubbed Animatronics, was developed by Jim Henson's Creature Shop.

Jim Henson
The creator of the Muppets and the voice of Kermit the Frog, Jim Henson (1937–1990) directed a number of films, including The Dark Crystal *(1982) (top left).*

Gremlins
The nasty little creatures from Gremlins *(1984) are spawned by a teenager's unusual new pet. The director, Steven Spielberg, had a small part in the film.*

Turtletronics

Computers enable a single puppeteer to control all the facial expressions of one of the famous Teenage Mutant Ninja Turtles. The mouth can be moved in a lifelike way by several motors and the eyes can open and

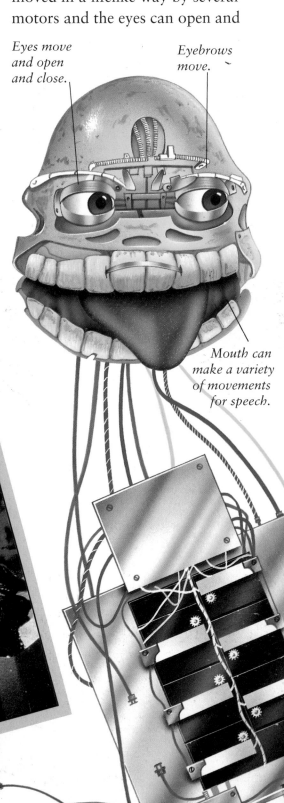

Eyes move and open and close.

Eyebrows move.

Mouth can make a variety of movements for speech.

The powerpack (right) with motors and radio control was hidden in the turtle's shell.

close, move left and right and up and down. The eyebrows move independently. Each of the turtles has two heads. One is packed with Creature Shop electronics to bring the face to life. The other is a stunt head with a fixed expression used in long shots and other scenes where movement is not necessary. To ensure a perfect fit, Creature Shop technicians made casts of the actors' bodies before making the costumes.

The mask covering the mechanics is made of highly flexible foam rubber.

Two Velociraptors look menacing in Steven Spielberg's Jurassic Park.

Pesky Penguins

In *Batman Returns* (1992), the villainous Penguin's army consisted of real penguins, actors in glass fiber suits, animatronic puppets controlled by puppeteers under the set, and computer animation. A technique called flocking was used where several penguins would imitate a master penguin. This allowed control over large numbers.

Dinomania

In *Jurassic Park* (1993), the terrifying dinosaurs exist courtesy of the computer. For some close-up shots, like the scene in which a T-rex takes a bite out of a station wagon, latex and rubber models were used. But the movie also contains 54 sequences, totaling nearly seven minutes, in which the dinosaurs are entirely computer generated. The computer animators have 16.7 million shades to match the colors in modern film, right down to the mud on the back of a Velociraptor.

COMPUTERS

Computer Revolution

State-of-the-art computer technology is changing the face of special effects. What are known as "digital effects," stored in the memory banks of computers, can be used to manipulate movie images in ever more weird and wonderful ways. The first film to make extensive use of computers was Disney's *Tron* (1982), in which Jeff Bridges found himself inside a computer. In 1984 the science fiction movie *The Last*

Computer Animator
A team of 40 animators and computer programmers worked on the digital special effects for Terminator 2.

Starfighter created spaceships in the computer, using technology developed by the United States Army. But the big breakthrough came with *Terminator 2* (1991) in which computer power originally developed for engineering design and flight simulators was harnessed to make the seemingly impossible happen.

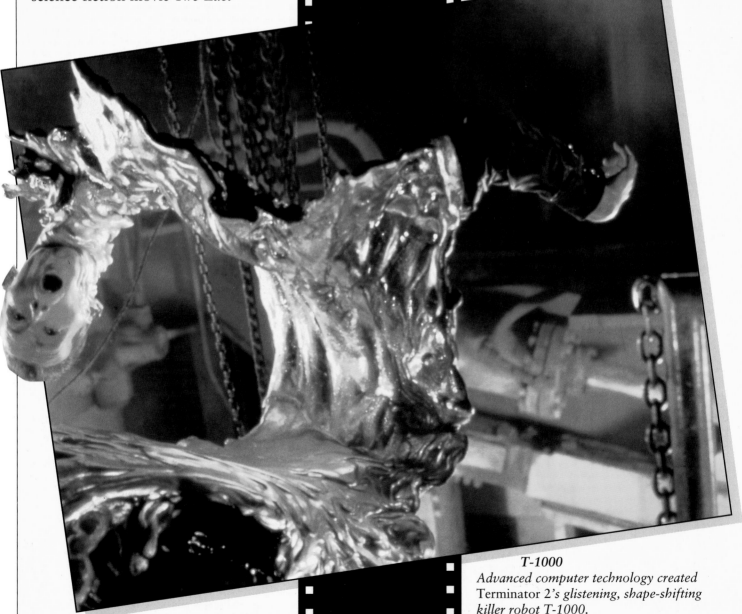

T-1000
Advanced computer technology created Terminator 2's *glistening, shape-shifting killer robot T-1000.*

Computer Monsters
Some of the hordes of dinosaurs in Jurassic Park (1993) were computer-generated as this sequence left shows. The actor plays the scene running from the imaginary beast. T-Rex was then built up using a powerful graphics computer. The final shot shows the finished scene, which combines the two separate images at the film editing stage. And very believable it is too!

Optical Printer

The bag of tricks known as the optical printer has been with us longer than computers. A combination of camera and projector facing each other, it can produce such special effects as slow motion.

Morphing

T-1000 was produced by a process known as "morphing." A 2-inch grid is drawn over a real actor. His face is then laser-scanned and his movements filmed for conversion into a computer model capable of being moved in and out of the live action.

ANIMATION—COMPUTER
ANIMATION AND CLAYMATION

Animation is the most flexible film medium. If you can draw it or move it, you can animate it. Cinema audiences were enjoying short animated films in the early 1900s, but it was not until 1937 that Walt Disney produced the first feature-length cartoon, *Snow White and the Seven Dwarfs*. Now, after a period in the doldrums, cartoons are back with a vengeance. In 1993 the biggest movie hit was the Disney animated feature *Aladdin,* which made well over $200 million in America alone. A new generation of animators making stunning use of computer graphics had ushered in a new age of animation.

Cel, cel, cel!
The basis of animation is the cel, a celluloid sheet on which cartoon animators draw foreground action. There is one cel for every film frame but animation artists concentrate on the so-called "key frames," where movement begins and ends.

Cartoon King
In 1928 animator Walt Disney created one of the famous figures in film, Mickey Mouse. Mickey was soon joined by a menagerie of animal characters, among them Minnie Mouse, Donald Duck, Pluto and Goofy. Disney followed the success of the feature-length Snow White and the Seven Dwarfs *(1937) with a string of cartoon classics, including* Pinocchio *(1940) and* 101 Dalmatians *(1961).*

Hold It Down
Animated films are shot frame by frame with a rostrum camera. The rostrum is a small platform with legs on top of which the camera is mounted. During photography it provides rigid support for the camera and the animation board beneath it, which holds the artwork to be photographed. The animation camera, which can be moved up and down, is fitted with a stop-motion motor so that it can photograph each tiny animated movement frame by frame.

Felix the Cat
This 1991 version of Felix the Cat was based on the original introduced in 1914. Felix reached the height of his fame in the 1920s, but was eclipsed by the arrival of Mickey Mouse.

George Sanders
Cartoon characters must have the right voice. Suave George Sanders voiced the tiger Sheer Khan in The Jungle Book.

Robin Williams
One of the finest comic actors in Hollywood, Robin Williams voiced the motormouth genie in the smash-hit Disney cartoon version of Aladdin.

Missing Links
In an animated feature like *Watership Down* (1978), shown below, work begins with pencil and paper sketches made by the lead animators, who draw the characters in a variety of poses. The sketches go to a "clean-up artist" who produces individual

frames with clear lines. These are used by the inkers and painters to produce the final image on the cels. Each character also has several "in-betweeners" who link "key frames."

Fern Gully: The Last Rainforest
This beautifully animated film with an ecological message made extensive use of computer techniques.

Make Your Own Flicker Book
Cut out several pieces of paper to the same size. Draw a simple image on one piece and then trace it on the next piece making a small change. Repeat this until the story is complete and staple them together. Flick through to watch your very own animation!

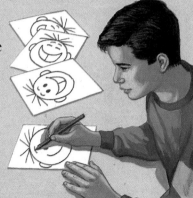

Computer Animation

In *Aladdin* a computer was used to create the twisting and turning patterns on Aladdin's flying carpet. First, a single head-on view of the pattern was painted. This was scanned into a computer which distorted it to match the outlines of the animator's drawings. Finally it was "tweaked" by a computer graphics expert who gave it shadows for a three-dimensional appearance.

Computer Help

One important role for the computer in animation is that of "extra pencil." Animators still create characters with a pencil but a computer can speed up the process between "key frames." Computers also give animators greater control of the camera, and the clever use of computer graphics technology can give them complete command over the three dimensions.

The artist draws the beginning and end.

The computer fills in the animation.

Bob and the Baby Bob Hoskins faces the cigar-chomping, starlet-chasing Baby Herman in Who Framed Roger Rabbit? *(1988).*

Invisible Joins

Live action has been combined with animation in many films. Dick van Dyke and Julie Andrews frolicked with cartoon animals in *Mary Poppins* (1964) and Gene Kelly danced with Tom and Jerry in *Anchors Aweigh* (1943). But in *Who Framed Roger Rabbit?* (1988) director Robert Zemeckis and his animators merged live and cartoon action so brilliantly that the joins are impossible to see. The movie was

Duet for One
In the live scenes, Bob Hoskins acted facing thin air—so how did he duck Roger in a dishwasher and watch the rabbit come up spitting water? He was filmed with a spigot which squirted water at the height of Roger's head. Then animators drew the cartoon over the spigot.

Bob Hoskins clutches the spigot in live action.

Roger is cartooned over the spigot with his mouth puckered in the same place as the nozzle.

made in three stages. First the live action scenes were filmed in Los Angeles. In the second part the animation was done in England, at Elstree studios, under the supervision of Richard Williams. In the third part the special effects team at Industrial Light and Magic brought Bob Hoskins and Roger Rabbit together. The making of the movie involved just about every known technique of visual effects, and many new ones invented to cope with the demands of the project and to make two separate movies into one.

Animators
Traditional animation is created by large groups of animators drawing individual frames on clear cels. But more and more animators are using computers.

Animation and reality face each other in a scene from Volere Volare *(1992) in which a man who works in a film-dubbing studio finds himself turning into a cartoon.*

Stop and Go

Stop-motion animation is a simple but time-consuming method of animating three-dimensional objects, in which the camera is operated one frame at a time. In between each frame the object is slightly adjusted so that when you run the film at normal speed, the objects move. One of the supreme examples of stop-motion photography was *King Kong* (1933). The giant gorilla in the movie was in fact six 18-inch models.

Stop-motion Man
Animator Ray Harryhausen is the leading stop-motion man and inventor of Superdynamation.

Skeleton Dance

In the skeleton fight from Ray Harryhausen's *Jason and the Argonauts* (1963), the actor was filmed first and then the stop-motion skeletons animated in. The skeletons were 8-inch rubber models, and the five-minute scene took five months to film.

Claymation

On the set at Aardman Animation, stop-motion techniques are used to animate Plasticine figures built around flexible wire skeletons. The pioneer of Plasticine animation is Nick Park, who won an Oscar in 1989 for *Creature Comforts*.

① Miniature set
② Lights
③ Monitor
④ Video camera
⑤ Film camera
⑥ Models
⑦ Props

The Wrong Trousers

Wallace and Gromit the dog appeared in *The Wrong Trousers* (1993). During filming, the Plasticine models had to be resculpted after every movement as Plasticine tears slightly when moved. Mouths are particularly difficult to animate – in *The Wrong Trousers*, Wallace had to have several sets of teeth, each with a different width of grin. About a dozen different mouth shapes were used for when he spoke.

Plasticine Stars
Wallace and Gromit were the stars of A Grand Day Out.

Frame by Frame

Nick Park's films begin as a script which is then transferred to a storyboard. Every important frame of action is drawn and placed in sequence. The storyboard is also turned into an "animatic," a video film that stays on each frame of the storyboard for as long as the sequence will last in the finished film. When filming, it is vital to make sure that each figure stays in exactly the same position for each frame or it will appear to wobble about. So Park simultaneously shoots every frame with two cameras—a film camera and a single-frame video camera. The video image is stored in a computer so it can then be compared with the position of the figure in the next frame.

Talking Bears
These polar bears featured in Nick Park's Oscar-winning animated film Creature Comforts *(1989).*

Putting It All Together

The job of selecting, assembling and arranging the many different sequences of a film to tell a story is handled by the editor. Editing begins as soon as the first day's shooting is completed. Each day's printed footage, known as "rushes," is sent to the editor's workshop, the "cutting room." As the scenes are gradually pieced together, they become the "work print." When all the footage is "in the can" and arranged in more or less the right order, the editor begins the complicated task of trimming and shaping the film, with sound and special effects, first into a "rough cut" version , then a "fine cut" and finally a print approved by the director and producer.

The Editor
Some film directors always work with the same editor. Director Martin Scorsese's editor is Thelma Schoonmaker, who won an Oscar for Raging Bull (1981).

Clapper Board
The clapper board (see page 19) is important in the editing process. The editor marries up the clap on the sound track with the right frame on the film to ensure that sound and pictures are properly synchronized.

Making a Splash

Big films are launched with a première, a highly publicized special screening before an invited audience of celebrities. The most famous première of all was for *Gone With the Wind* on December 15, 1939 in the city of Atlanta, Georgia. Atlanta's population of 300,000 swelled to 1.5 million as huge crowds lined the streets to see the stars of the film parade in 50 cars garlanded with flowers.

Editing Table
On the editing table, the editor has a screen showing the action and a speaker playing the sound track. He slowly assembles the film, cutting it down to its final length.

Tape Splicer
This has a small cutting blade and is used to join film together. Small pins secure the film to cut between frames.

Adding Sounds
The picture and original sound track are synchronized, together with additional sound tracks, onto which background noises can be added.

THE COMMUNITY

Making a Killing

Producers can multiply their profits with film spin-offs. This is known as merchandizing—selling the film through toys, T-shirts, books and posters linked with the production.

Advertising Art
Posters play an important part in promoting a movie. Original posters for classic movies of the past are highly sought-after by collectors and change hands for large sums of money.

The Oscars

The most coveted prizes in the film world are handed out every year at the Academy Awards ceremony, a glittering occasion watched worldwide on television. The winners of the various categories—which include Best Actor, Actress and Picture—receive a small gold statuette known as an "Oscar." A Best Picture Oscar is a guarantee of success at the box office.

Into the Shops
Merchandising items for Jurassic Park (1993) have earned millions of extra dollars.

INDEX

Picture Credits
Abbreviations: t-top, m-middle, b-bottom, l-left, r-right
Cover, 28-29, 43, 48t: Warner Bros (Courtesy Kobal Collection); 6-7, 8r, 10-11: Kobal Collection; 9: Melies (Courtesy Kobal); 11m, 52: Carolco (Courtesy Kobal); 16-17, 51: Amblin/ Universal (Courtesy Kobal); 21 inset, 31: Columbia (Courtesy Kobal); 26: Edison (courtesy Kobal); 28b, 29b: United Artists (Courtesy Kobal); 30: 20th Century Fox/ Morgan Creek (Courtesy Kobal); 40: Societe Generale de Films/Gaumont/MGM (Courtesy Kobal); 42t: MGM (Courtesy Kobal); 46t: UFA (Courtesy Kobal); 46-47: Lucas Film/20th Century Fox (Courtesy Kobal); 55t & m: 20th Century Fox (Courtesy Kobal); 57b: Bambu/ Pentafilm (Courtesy Kobal); 58b: RKO (Courtesy Kobal); title p, 18-19: Panavision; 6: The National Museum of Photography, Film & Television (Courtesy the Science Museum, London); 81, 10m, 14t, 18m, 20t, 20-21, 22, 23 both, 24, 25, 32t, 34 both, 36, 37 both, 38 both, 39, 42b, 48b, 50b, 55m, 56-57, 58t, 59 all: The Ronald Grant Archive: 10b: Eric T Budge; 11t & b: The Handmade Film Partnership (Distributers) LTD; 14m, 26-27, 27t, 32m & b, 41, 44 both, 49, 50t, 60-61, 61b: Frank Spooner Pictures; 53 all: Copyright © by Universal Pictures, a Division of Universal City Studios, Inc. Courtesy of MCA Publishing Rights, a Division of MCA Inc.; 61t: Paul Nightingale.